SCISSORTAIL QUARTERLY

No. 01   November 2020

SCISSORTAIL PRESS
Stillwater, Oklahoma

Printed in the United States of America

ISBN: 979-8-5703-7681-6

Design by Brian Fuchs
Cover photo copyright © Brent Fuchs Photography

No. 01, November 2020

Scissortail Press
4500 E Burris Rd
Glencoe, OK 74032

www.scissortailpress.com
Instagram: @scissortailquarterly, @scissortail.press

"The other guys were older —
all i had
was energy & balls"

All i brought 2

CONTENTS

CHRISTIAN GARDUNO
DIRTY BLUE QUASARS 3

PALMER SMITH
A LIGHT READ 6

DARIEN LENCL
CRACKER-JACKS AND FORTUNE COOKIES 9
THE NATIVES ARE RESTLESS..12

LUKE EMSLEY
TODAY I DID NOTHING..16
SWING AND A MISS...17
PLANKTON:...18
MANCHESTER, 2019 - THE LAST DAY OF THE DECADE - 20
FIREFLIES 21

LORRAINE CAPUTO
SOMEPLACE ON THE PAMPAS 28
A DENALI SUMMER 29
AUTUMN PASSAGES 32

DEE ALLEN.
SAINT SIN 35
BRO WAY...38

MICHAEL BROCKLEY
BECOMING A READER 41
"FOR A DOLLAR, THIS POEM BETTER BE FUNNY. OR ODD"...42
YOU UNCOVER THE LOST SEASHELL...............................43

MAED RILL MONTE
SO THE ONE BOOKSTORE IN TOWN WENT BANKRUPT……......46

RP VERLAINE
FOR JESSE 50
SHIFTING OF SHAPES...51

KATRINA K GUARASCIO
NATURAL DISASTER..53
MY HEART 54
SCARS 56

NDABA SIBANDA
12 DAYS 59

A WHITTENBERG
HELD 62
PASSING AS A MULATTO 63

MIRIAM SAGAN
UNSEASONABLE..65

JUDE BRIGLEY
THYRATIA BATIS 68
KEEPER 69
EACH OF THEM COULD BE US 70
COMPLEXITY..72

ZUBAIR JAVAID
REMINDING THE GOD 75
ZAINAB WRITES FOR HER BELOVED POET: 78

MAEVE MCKENNA
BAT 81

JB MULLIGAN
PEOPLES IS A CURIOUS AMINAL...84

VEGETAL...86

ICHABOD'S PRIZE 88

JOHN LAMBREMONT
A MAN AND HIS MUSE 92

THE BACKWARD ATTACKER..93

LISHA RUAN
RIVER..96

FLOW 96

EMPTY...97

RACHEL DEVEREAUX
THERE WAS A BABY..100

AYESHA ASIM
FLYING...103

TIFFANY LINDFIELD
THE WIND SINGS 105

MARTINA GALLEGOS
DOUBLE-WHAMMY...108

A NATION ON EDGE 109

A NATION SIGHS A SIGH OF RELIEF.....................................110

BETTER LIFE MATTERS 111

CAN YOU HEAR ME? 113

DOUGLAS K CURRIER
REST,..116

A WAY THAT COUNTS 117

GEORGE HIGHAM

WANDERING FREE 120

JOHN CARTER

TURTLES 124

ANOTHER STAGE OF GRIEF 125

CHRISTIAN GARDUNO

Christian Garduno's work can be read in over 50 literary magazines, including *Riza Press*, where his poem, "The Return", was a Finalist in their 2019 Multimedia Contest. He lives and writes along the South Texas coast with his wonderful wife Nahemie and young son Dylan.

He sometimes usually writes at
https://medium.com/@letsfly2000

DIRTY BLUE QUASARS

Gauze of yellow light filtered through stained glass eyes
I've been staying up well past noon
staring out at the porcelain skies inside your room
you keep the trinkets of certain pilfered prophets
lol we all take our own chances, you wink
you've the dust of pandemia all across your skin
you're laugh is on loop in my mind like all the Rembrandts on
fire
you stumbled, trip, and flip, but never spill a drop of your
magnolia wine

One by one, stars go out
or do they just go on for someone else
you never ask these questions, draw a cubed pyramid
the signal's in the drying machine
when you time it just right
saints & souls
they go round after round
they push the sun above ground

Dirty blue quasars in the corner of her mouth
she takes her time on the letter V
your laugh in an echo chamber
it's an indictment unto itself

PALMER SMITH

Palmer Smith is a graduate of Sarah Lawrence College and an incoming MFA and MA student. She has worked as a paralegal since 2018. She has written for *Refresh Magazine*, *The Online Journal for Person-Centered Dermatology*, *Sea Maven Magazine*, *Calm Down Magazine*, *The French Press Zine* and *level:deepsouth*, with work forthcoming in The Remington Review and For Women Who Roar.

Instagram: @spdevsmith

A LIGHT READ

Shaking fingers at you invisibly,
shaking one at myself mirrored.
Yesterday half hanging body
curling kissing the rooftop fence
Down down deep down the taxis
swirling, not colliding yet,
Big plastic Dice twisted
reflected in the windshield,
 no destination.

Last Monday bathing lavender bubbles
soaking my skin. Hours Hours in the hours
sleeping, dreaming of purple Nightmares,
turning brain off, on, off, on.
Accepting static sounds.

I heard the brain continues to hear for minutes after.

Tomorrow corner of 86th and Madison
a traveler crosses.
No patience for the electronic go,
Body struck and flying in dark-hell pants
and worn-rotted loafers.

One loafer hits opposite side of sidewalk.

Rain.

Rain.

Rain.

Weeks later many signs:
Did you see the car that killed our mother?

(And didn't kill me.)

DARIEN LENCL

Darien Lencl lives in the San Francisco Bay Area. Concrete disquiets him, but he dwells with cities none-the-less. He is sad to leave the mountains and forests when the camping is done, but happy to be home when the rubber of tires touches the pavement of a driveway. He has featured at the several Bay Area poetry shows, as well as the prestigious "Passages on the Lake" show. He has been a teacher in Oakland for over 20 years, and has been performing poetry in Oakland since 2000.

Darien has been writing poetry for 25 years. He tries to mitigate life's abundance with moderation, but ends up being more apt with, "if a little is good, then a lot is better." As he has gotten older, he has realized that this is unfolding folly. For, much in the world tries to communicate that less is more. That being said, he still prefers three friends to two, and where Ice cream is concerned, an extra scoop.

CRACKER-JACKS AND FORTUNE COOKIES

Not much surprises me.
Spontaneity,
mitigated by monotony.
The same route everyday.
So, I go left, instead of right —
Several stop signs,
instead of a stoplight.
At the first,
there is an elderly man with cane
whose slow creaky gait
held me just long enough
to have a mother and her circus of 3 boys,
cross the street in front of me.

One was, eyes to the sky-chasing a butterfly,
the other was chasing his brother —
And the youngest,
bent down to pick up something shiny.
He examined it —
Oblivious to my car.
It was a pint-sized army guy.
Why am I not surprised?

At the next stop sign,
a man was selling newspapers.
I saw the front page:
Young, Black, BART, Murdered, Nia.
I looked at the big photo,

and saw an image of my student
from last school-year.
Nia Wilson:
In class, she could be a handful
or a whisper.
I found myself wishing
that she could have been more
of a whisper on that BART train; invisible;
just part of a seat.
She may very well have been.
Though, it didn't stop some crazy man
from stabbing her in the throat.
Still, I wasn't surprised.
Our diet is violence.

My current thoughts made me mindful of appreciation.
I was surprised at how easy it is,
to not see my mother.
She lives not two exits away.
So, I turned my car towards the freeway,
and paid my mother a visit.
Years of opiates and reality T.V.
have turned her into one of the cushions on the couch,
but she was happy to see me —
And some cushions give the best support.
We talked and watched T.V.
Channel 2 had on the news.
Nia's story came up.
They flashed a photo of her holding a gun.
I wasn't surprised.
KTVU is a Fox affiliate.

I told my mother that I was hungry
and going to get food.
She didn't want any, but said,
"Here honey. Take this,"
and handed me a box of Cracker Jacks.
I ate them, but there was no surprise inside.
So, I went to get some Chinese food—
Figuring the fortune, inside of the fortune-cookie,
would make up for the Cracker Jack mishap.
And sure enough,
after the noodles and rice were gone—
I opened a fortune cookie
and there was a fortune inside.
It said:
The world is full of surprises,
but you have to allow yourself to get excited.
Just then, my favorite teacher,
from when I was in high school, walked in.
I was so excited to see her.
I told her about my day.
She said, She could relate.

THE NATIVES ARE RESTLESS

Here, upon this land, the restless walk
with nervous knees and bouncing feet
upon a concrete that covers the soil —
A source, for the restless,
of countenance and toil —
Who for years, have preferred
the churn in the turn
of cogs in a machine —
Sending human beings,
on a restless quest, for oil.

Here, upon this land,
the restless walk —
Flocking to their jobs;
their institutions; their endeavors —
Paying no attention to the mirror
provided by seagulls circling overhead —
Waiting in restless circles
for us to be dead; to be food —
Ruined, by the earnest and erstwhile inertia
of our errands —
Driving the clock of our dissolution
closer to the strike of our midnight demise.

Here, upon this land,
where the restless walk —
There is a history of genocide;
of bloodshed;
of a filthy pilfering
from our Earth and spirits;

from our flesh and bone;
from the substances that form faith, save grace,
and attenuate the sacred with taste.
We are left with an alienating chasm
to pour our energies into,
as it spasms into an unquenchable consumption-
Keeping our best future from view.

Here, upon this land,
where the restless walk —
the original inhabitants
have been reduced to trinkets in art stores;
to images contained in frames on gallery walls;
to smiling mascots embossed across
professional sports paraphernalia;
Natives, reduced to fashion accessories;
to playing cards; to bubble gum.
An entire Native people
reduced to an idealized, romanticized myth,
by a dispossessing nation-
manifest, in its destiny —
Trying desperately to bleach the blood
from the relentless restlessness in its conscious.

LUKE EMSLEY

Luke is a poet, spoken-word artist and rapper. Having originally trained as an actor at London's Italia Conti Academy, Luke is highly passionate about the power of the spoken word; he is fascinated with the use of rhythm, after becoming spellbound by Shakespeare's use of iambic pentameter: it was a foregone conclusion that Luke would look to immerse himself in poetry and performance! His first venture into the world poetic was when penning marketing verses for his debut novel Beyond Daylight. The poetry soon took on a life of its own and Luke hasn't looked back. He will be publishing his first collection of poetry in 2021 as well and releasing a debut rap EP. Much of his poetry can be found on Instagram (under the handle @l_3_m_s_l_3_y).

TODAY I DID NOTHING

didn't lift even a finger

netflix skipped through the hours -
documentaries on deranged minds

and I sat, doing nothing,
like a tin-can not worth even a kick
and I just sat, as by me and through me,
moments ate moments
ate moments ate

like self-consuming serpents

and amidst
this writhing mass of moments (once alive now
already dead)
I sat and
did nothing at all

and somewhere, a heavy smoker
laughed
a rattling, rasping
laugh

SWING AND A MISS

My remedy is beer,
'cos private therapy is too dear.
I'm self-medicating;
I should be meditating.
Apparently, my choices are clearly indicating
PSYCHOSIS
on the deepest of levels.
I might look fine but my mind's dishevelled.
A medical professional
made the maze
and now I'm stuck in this
malevolent malaise.
So please excuse the vacant look on my face,
when you tell me to calm down and behave.
Just gimme my pills;
gimme my spade;
and I'll be off outside to
dig my own grave.

PLANKTON:

[noun]

1. The aggregate of passively floating, drifting, or somewhat
motile organisms occurring in a body of water, primarily
comprising microscopic
algae and protozoa.

Out of sight,
the wide-eyed whale,
that lunatic leviathan
glides heavy,
stays the course and
rolls
through dark oceans
in which few dare drift.

Out of sight, then, and
unshackled by all that is considered the norm,
this vast and utterly
mad finbackyawns: it makes
banking algorithms skip
and air traffic control desk safety lights blink
and previously steadfast scientific principles
shrink and shudder then
rip.

And in dark oceans,
the mad whale's jaws part and a canyon-like
vacuum
awakens into which tonne after tonne after

tonne of plankton slip,
and then simply no longer exist.

PLANKTON:

[noun]

2. A metaphorical mass-noun used to symbolise the
overwhelming multitudes that have mistaken choices borne of
fear for logic and pragmatism.

3. Any person/s that believe happiness comes from middling
ambition and underwhelming material possessions.

4. Something that will, at any moment, inconsequentially vanish,
without trace, as if unceremoniously swallowed.

MANCHESTER, 2019 - THE LAST DAY OF THE DECADE -

and a six-year old kid kicks
a laughing-gas can along pot-holed roads.
Beneath furious murals,
a homeless waif swallows the
public's refusals
to spare any change
with a grim dignity.

A supercar prowls by,
it growls like

we're naught but carrion.

FIREFLIES

...punk-broke
I drunk-drove
through the night
to flee from that ebon horse that grew in my
rearview mirror every time I snatched a
glance back:
just a black, massive menace.

It had galloped rough-shod
over the burning horizons of my past, and
bore down now, hell-bent on crushing my future
beneath cast-iron and blood-mired hooves
the likes of which
I hope you'll never need know.

But then, somewhere between the Sculpture
Park and despair, in the
cool amber aura of the dashboard,
I noted, amongst the car-wired lights,

two fireflies.

Now cars by night emit eldritch light -
dials and meters and warning signs;
these fireflies were easily lost in the
luminescence, especially to maddened eyes,
such as were mine, that night.
But I found myself wanting to watch for them

those sparkling little darts in the dark.

And why not?
I could focus either on the flies or otherwise
on the thunderous crescendo of the
nightmare mare's hooves hammering over all
hope just a little way behind us on the
weeping wet road —

wait - — 'us?'
The fireflies and I -
what of this then: this new 'us'...?

"Avoid bridges," the fireflies told me, "let us
lead you away from bridges and away from
walls. Let us ease your feet; soften a little your
speed.
Don't fear the charge of the dark steed;
just listen; and let us lead
you to...

...a behemoth-big bean
bag, not long later; it envelops me like a
womb and here I find safety and sleep and
tea - and more fireflies!

They flutter in kind eyes that don't show
alarm as I offload my burdens like boulders
and lay them out like the end of the road.

Come morning, I see fireflies - everywhere!

I see fireflies in the kettle light's boil light.

Fireflies in the glistening of sizzling bacon.
Fireflies in the fizzing effervescence
of a hangover-tablet that pukes
upward-fumes of fuchsia and vitality into a
glass of water.
Fireflies rest on the arms of a
sofa and in the charging-light of the PS4 and by
kettlebells and kit that only the strongest
of men can lift.

They are everywhere!

Here, in this suburb of Wakefield; in Durkar, and Denby
Dale too. They populate all the boroughs of
Barnsley and the 5k hospital halls not far from
from Hibaldstow. There are fireflies in
maternity wards in Watford; and in Bradford
tattoo parlours. There are fireflies in late night
bowling alleys in NYC; they dance in the
tornadoes of storm-torn Lake Charles; and in
Malaysian high-rises, so far from home; they
glow sombre and lovely 'neath melancholy clouds
in busy Coloradan supermarkets; they beam in
golden-sand smiles on Egyptian beaches;
they love the whirring of treadmills in West
Yorkshire gyms; and somewhere, not far from
Moscow, in rural Russia, there too the fireflies -
they sing.

...and that's the thing about fireflies:
they're always there.
Even in the thickest of fogs when you've lost

sight of your heart and your road to hope,
they're there.

Somewhere close.

If you just learn to look and learn to see.

There's another thing about fireflies too:
remember that most dire of nags
(that you yourself broke in and trained
and raised to race and raze all beneath those
bludgeoner's hooves)
that corpse-horse that thunders through the
blackest of longest of nights, well it's
terrified of fireflies.

Really fucking shit-the-bed scared of fireflies.

So if your world ever darkens
and the sounds of wild whinnying
start hissing through the trees,
and that clip-clop canter picks up the gallop,
look for me.

Because -

I love you

and because, like countless,
countless

others,
I am
and will forever be
for you

a firefly

just let yourself look… then… see!

LORRAINE CAPUTO

Lorraine Caputo is a documentary poet, translator and travel writer. Her works appear in over 180 journals on six continents; and 12 chapbooks of poetry – including *Caribbean Nights* (Red Bird Chapbooks, 2014), *Notes from the Patagonia* (dancing girl press, 2017) and *On Galápagos Shores* (dancing girl press, 2019). She also authors travel narratives, articles and guidebooks. In March 2011, the Parliamentary Poet Laureate of Canada honored her verse. Caputo has done over 200 literary readings, from Alaska to the Patagonia. She travels through Latin America, listening to the voices of the pueblos and Earth.

Follow her travels at:
www.facebook.com/lorrainecaputo.wanderer.

Website: http://latinamericawanderer.wordpress.com/

SOMEPLACE ON THE PAMPAS

I awaken
     someplace
         in the midst
     of emerald pampas
Sparse trees
     yet ebony
         silhouettes
     against
The sky
     just bluing
         with twilight
     of morn
& this day's sun
     rising in brilliant
         carmine & yellow
     orange & violet

A DENALI SUMMER

30 June
After a rain, hard and cold, sleet and hail, I peak between the branches of my refuge between, beneath twin elder spruce trees.

The mist rises, twin rainbows rise from a valley, rise above jade-greened mountainsides still streaked with snow, rise into clouds.

13 August
The magenta stars of fireweed flowers have long reached the top of their long stems—A warning the snows will arrive in five weeks . . . so the old-timers say.

In the chilling western wind the cinnamon-gold lance leaves stand stiff. The feathery white seeds drift past. Heavy grey clouds fill the valley.

15 August
For several weeks the clouds have buried the mountains. In the almost constant drizzle, we watch the fireweed seeds flurry by, we watch those clouds form and flow.

Finally this evening they parted. Far to the south, the Alaska Range was streaked, from peak down through valleys, with fresh snow.

A light rain began again in the evening sun. Across the sky, from one deep valley to another beneath the newly white mountains, arched a rainbow.

18 August
At mid-summer, the sun swooped behind those northern mountains, leaving us in twilight for a short while. Then he would reëmerge, bringing the long days of light.

But now the sun circles further and further southward. The days grow shorter. True night has begun to settle. Stars appear in the blackness. The Aurora sheets the sky in waving curtains of color.

21 August
I walk through the taiga on a once-again-born night glowing with the Light and meteorites. All around the owls speak from a tree to my right, another further to the left.

Out on the northern ridge, a coyote answers his brother. I stop to listen and yip a greeting. Their replies come clearly through the dark.

An Arctic wind blows from those mountains with the icy smell of snow.

23 August
On this, a frosty morning after a night of the Northern Lights dancing green in the starry sky, dancing with the Milky Way and shooting stars, after that evening's alpenglow faded away on the mountains ringing this valley, mountains topped with freshly fallen snow …

On this frosty morning, I sit here and wonder if this is really August.

3 September

I awaken to the brightness of light reflected off a virgin bed of snow.

All day, those large clusters of flurries blinded this valley. All day, we trudged through the thickening blanket, doing our work.

Near dinnertime, it stopped with silence. Eighteen inches of heavy wet snow now mound this land. It has finally touched us in this lowland.

7 September

Through this warmish and wet night chilled with frost, an owl song travels through the spruce and aspen. Across this dripping sky, clouds layer grey and rose.

Weaving down moose trails, I sidestep puddles reflecting the sky and trees.

The horns of the passing freight train echo heavy and clear through this valley. The weight of its tanker cars rumbles the earth.

AUTUMN PASSAGES

I.

Rose madder bleeds through
    fall monsoon clouds, seeps across
        the ragged grey dawn.
    A lone crow caws, slicing the
quiet gathering sunlight.

A stalk of foxtail
    dances its fattened seed head
        in the pallid breeze.

Waves of bronze starlings
    swoop over dried grassy fields,
        perch on sycamores.

II.

Burnished oak leaves float
    upon cold-thickened waters
        and choke a thin stream
    meandering through a copse
of bare trees and frozen earth.

Frosted blue berries
    bunch densely, they hang heavy
        on jade cedar boughs.

III.

By late afternoon
    tarnished rain splatters upon
        harvest-gold meadows
    dappled with scarlet sumac.
Icy gusts whirl leaves and earth.

Geese huddle in the
    marshes of a lake scattered
        with fractured sunlight.

First fragile flakes fall
    swirling on sharp winds whistling
        through brittle-leafed limbs.

DEE ALLEN.

African-Italian performance poet based in Oakland, California. Active on the creative writing & Spoken Word tips since the early 1990s. Author of 5 books [*Boneyard*, *Unwritten Law*, *Stormwater*, and *Skeletal Black*, all from POOR Press, and his newest from Conviction 2 Change Publishing, *Elohi Unitsi*] and 28 anthology appearances [including *Your Golden Sun Still Shines*, *Rise*, *Extreme*, *The Land Lives Forever*, *Civil Liberties United*, *Trees In A Garden Of Ashes* and the newest, *Colossus: Home*] under his figurative belt so far.

SAINT SIN

Saint. Sin.
Saint Sin.
Two little words
That don't belong
On the same name.

Saint. Sin.
Saint Sin.
First name: Siren.
Lifted from the singing
Mermaids of Greek-Roman myth

Thousands of sailors
Lured by their song to the rocky
Seashore, to their deaths.
She has the same effect
Minus the fatal implications.

Saint. Sin.
Saint Sin.
Two little words
That spell out
Dichotomy.

Nice and naughty.
Implied combination
Recalling another
Acclaimed brunette
We all used to know.

Saint. Sin.
Saint Sin.
For alternative models,
Possible patron saint.
For everyone else,

The voluptuous, tattooed,
Burlesque, webcam saint.
Our Lady
Of Lust
Inducement.

Saint. Sin.
Saint Sin.
Someone else
Lingers within her,
Besides her.

Bettie Page's spirit
Lives inside her bones and
Decorative white skin, it seems—
At the right time, she emerges from
Marrow and joints, makes her host dominant or playful.

Saint. Sin.
Saint Sin.
Curvy pale vixen refines
The life she enjoys, becomes
The fantasy enjoyed by others.

More than a model in lace lingerie,
More than a subject in tight black leather,

El Paso's Goddess Of Tease does well in
Capturing her person in a tiny camera lens—
Maybe Bunny Yeager lives on in her also—

BRO WAY

Redacted documents exist,
But do redacted road signs?

One sure enough does
In these smoky and pestilent times.

Splotch of Krylon© black
Spray-paint changes the name
And character of downtown
Oakland's main drag

From Broadway
To Bro Way and it shows.

When the businesses closed down
Behind thick plywood and nails,
Polychromatic murals went up,
Coating them with words and images.
Open air, free of charge
Art exhibit over two blocks wide.

Aerosol can-made homages
To the non-Caucasians no longer here —
Bayard Rustin, Ray Charles, John Lewis, Sandra Bland,
Emmett Till, George Floyd, Breonna Taylor —
And heroes still
Among the living —
Angela Davis, Cornel West, Boots Riley, Stevie Wonder —

Different sceneries in different hues declare

Liberation for the Africans here in the West.
The dead deserve justice,
The living, respect —

Who would've thought civil unrest,
Shattered windows, protestors battling cops,

Could bring a great surfeit
Of beautiful paint, art for blocks?

MICHAEL BROCKLEY

Michael Brockley is a retired school psychologist who lives in Muncie, Indiana. His most recent poems have appeared in *Last Stanza*, *Unbroken*, and *The Thieving Magpie*. Poems are forthcoming in *Flying Island*, the *Indianapolis Anthology*, and the anthology *What Was and What Will Be*.

BECOMING A READER

I don't remember where I put the clothes I kept on hangers, but I began reading To Russia, With Love in the back bedroom of a house that straddled the border between my hometown and the country. I no longer pretended to be a priest who consecrated marbles in a cherry tobacco chalice at the altar of my dresser. Instead I egged my brother into arguing that a blonde who lost her husband to an actress with violet eyes was more beautiful than a brunette with Mickey Mouse ears. I watched the world through that bedroom window. The capture of an escaped bull, the mourning of a stranded goose, circus trains braking at the entrance to the 4-H park. The stained bed sheets strung across the clothes line that cut our yard in half. I used the flashlight I hid under the bed to read about the Baseball Hall of Fame and Roy Chapman Andrews' All About Strange Beasts of the Past. Plastic statues of the Virgin Mary and the Sacred Heart bookended two shoeboxes of paperbacks stacked at the back of my dresser. Haphazardly crammed with For Your Eyes Only and The Spy Who Loved Me and Goldfinger. The Everyman's Library edition of Edgar Allen Poe plus a dog-eared copy of Grifter's Game. I slept in a narrow bed over a plastic bedwetter's pad. Sometimes I left a brown stegosaurus or a green army man with a melted bazooka on the floor overnight. I never changed the batteries in my flashlight.

"FOR A DOLLAR, THIS POEM BETTER BE FUNNY, OR ODD"

A Bard's on the Run Poem for Carisa

I get gussied up in rainbows like a Woodstock mama with too many cats. My Weimaraner raises a ruckus over any hint of mint in my gingersnaps. Yet Baskerville can't scare the bejesus out of the Latter-day Saints before they ruin my morning sleep-ins with their spiel about marrying a Mormon. I dig jams where guitarists shred with their teeth. No unbroken circles for these ears. No stand by your man. Before breakfast, I melt Tammy Wynette 45s like Salvador Dalí liquidating clocks. On the other hand, 1910 novels about butter pecan ice cream perch at the top of my Saturday-night-and-no-Nicholas-Cage-flick-to-watch list. I'm a pushover for the schemes of robber barons. And a lady's man named Mr. Polly or Mr. Psmith buckles my knees. My life is a series of non sequiturs. Bipedal rhinoceroses lean against my car doors when I'm in the mood for an impulse tattoo. Miniature bicycles pedaled by French kings and queens circle my blue baby grand. In moments like these, I wonder what kind of flavor Superman ice cream is. I'm not from around here, but I guarantee I can do three sit ups with my eyes closed. My name is an unfinished sentence.

YOU UNCOVER THE LOST SEASHELL

while rearranging baseball novels on a bookshelf// the poet laureate of middle america gave you the conch as a writing prompt in the basement of a landmark church// ~~your country began ripping children away from their mothers then// and tossing them into dog cages where the guards urged them to drink from toilets//~~ the seashell reminds you of a carnotaurus with its beige and brown shading and its tiara of horns// the absence of embryonic feathers// the shell's low profile among the books written by malamud and kinsella resembles an armadillo's shuffle while anticipating its fright leap before onrushing traffic// an armadillo ranging into unknown territory unconcerned with its strange diet of jewel-backed beetles and the bayou taste of carpenter ants scurrying beneath an anonymous constellation// this is the seashell of armored creatures// oysters and sea urchins// the chainmail you have taken to wearing like a poor hex against your fears// ~~judges now tear out the wombs of women who seek refuge while wearing the wrong skins//~~ when you press the seashell to your ear you will hear the ravening of a black hole devouring what was once a star

MAED RILL MONTE

Maed Rill Monte's time is spent writing poetry and thinking of Jesus. He is 19 and has been published or forthcoming in *Anti-Heroin Chic, Strukturriss, Feral,* and elsewhere.

Facebook: https://www.facebook.com/maedrill.monte.31

SO THE ONE BOOKSTORE IN TOWN
WENT BANKRUPT...

I remember the interior
proportioned for
      pixies & dwarves
It was just that narrow: four walls slick with white
paint and right above the shelves was a Dr Seuss quote

To the right was the city telephone company
(on the first floor)   Top of it was a hip
karaoke bar where the college kids
partied in between semesters with
   pale pilsens & Hawaiian pizzas

I remember the signboard.
One could've never noticed walking across Zamora
Or riding a tricycle sitting on the steel edge of the front seat
a butt-cheek threatening
      to slide away to the concrete of the road
I mean I knew I should've told the bulb-eyed clerk or fixed the
thing myself
(for payment of a personal pick of one of those luxurious
Paul Coelho collection that lined across the top-shelf over
volumes
of folklore & arithmetic)

It was a pitiful signboard
    Hung up too high   Too
lofty for a small province-city
to take seriously.

It was the signboard.
Man, how I knew
it was the signboard —

RP VERLAINE

Rp Verlaine lives and writes in New York City. He has an MFA in creative writing from City College. He taught in New York Public schools for many years. Retired from teaching, he continues to write and do photography in New York. He had a volume of poetry- Damaged by Dames & Drinking published in 2017 and another – Femme Fatales Movie Starlets & Rockers in 2018. A set of three e books began with the publication of Lies From The Autobiography vol1 in November of 2018. Vol 2 was published in 2019 and a third Volume in 2020.

His poetry has appeared in *Atlas Poetica, The Linnet's Wings, Haikuniverse, Last Stanza Poetry Journal, The Local Train, Proletaria, Scryptic, Humankind Journal, The Wild Word, Under The Basho, Plum Tree Tavern, Fresh Out Magazine, Ugly Writers, Prune Juice, Incense Dreams, Best Poetry, Blazevox, Pikers Press, Poems' bout Love & Hate* anthology. *Stardust Haiku, Fractured Haiku, Scry of Lust 2.*

Facebook:
https://www.facebook.com/Rp-Verlaine-1552867308091481/

FOR JESSE

I saw you test irrelevant men
walking first avenue with
1 expletive. nuanced strides
and foreboding steps
disarming 3 cat callers
those hollow tongued verbal rapists
all swallowed their words
like amateurs doing Shakespeare
effectively neutered till you passed
and I totally fell in love with you
from the safe and silent distance
such things require.

SHIFTING OF SHAPES

Dawn
even when
circles square away
from
each obtuse
angle
the mind
still
validates the heart
as
your memory
rounds the
ellipse.

KATRINA K GUARASCIO

Katrina K Guarascio is an educator, writer, publisher, artist, and community organizer.

A lifelong creator, she has been published in various ezines, magazines, and anthologies. She also spent time on the performance stage, touring across the country in 2011 and participating in NPS in 2015, before hanging up her microphone. She is the author of two chapbook collections, two out of print collections, and three current books through Swimming with Elephants Publications, LLC.

Katrina lives gratefully and happily in New Mexico with the love of her life. She continues to write, perform, and publish her own writing on the website Flower and Sun (https://ironandsulfur.com/).

NATURAL DISASTER

tangled up from the twist
of tornado, all the best
parts of your disaster
rest, stone upon stone.
we curled ourselves into one.
limp bodies piled into hills
of the dead, I couldn't
unwrap all your thoughts of
me as quickly as you shake
the keys of untuned piano.
your eyes are still watching
for an unnamed god, your chin
held determined to the upcoming
wind. I got you on my back
watching moves and licking lips.
You sing the chimes from too
sore lips, cracked and chapped
my words blown out of portion.

MY HEART

with apologizes to Stephen Crane

he said it was
my heart
but I
ate of it regardless
and I drank each
drop with desperate
truth over sour
tongue.
a heart
must be consumed
become
part of me
and yet
and yet and yet and yet
I do not recognize
the taste. I am malnourished
and I know only the
hollow.
all their eyes
look the same and I
boil in fever.
all their
bones and their reasons
for love, what can one
person do to stay sane.
the rage passed and I am a
railroad so eager
to cut through, to
travel the transatlantic.

it is not logical
to traffic in wants,
but I am so hungry.
I slip inside cocoon,
a meditation,
I will mortgage
my future for the satisfaction
of a kind word and a tender
moment.
every day is precious
so let me wrap you in the chill
of morning;
it never takes
me more than
a bite or two.

SCARS

All his ticks are back,
the twitch in his left eye,
the flinch from chest to wrist.
He says he just needed a little bit of you,
is that ok?
just a little bit.
He shifts his eyes across hardwood,
crosses weathered arms,
letting storm beat spine.
You let him rest his head,
place a hand against closed eye,
to sooth the tremble.
He says he's sorry,
he just couldn't go through
another night of drinking alone.
He says he has nowhere else to go.
Watching the cracks of him swell,
you're reminded of his nightmares,
of the only other time you saw him cry.
Two in the morning on a Tuesday
when he confessed his sins.
He didn't cry when you left.
You cradle him through his downpour.
You invite him to stay,
offer coffee,
an ear,
what else can you give.
You tell him he doesn't have to go.
He puts on a strange half grin
wraps back around you,
burying his head in undone hair.

You soak up this unending stream
that has flooded living room
with tissued touch and whispered hush.
He holds you
with so much strength
your bones might snap.
He whispers, "you,"
whispers "girl,"
your name,
calls you "angel."
He hangs his head,
turns to the door,
tells you
he loves you
still.
Wrecked for rest,
you watch him leave you alone.
With empty hands you lock
the door behind him.
Surround by sudden silence,
you do the only thing you can think.
Put water on to boil for a bath,
find a cigarette butt
spoiled from another man's lips.
Take two drags,
the only two that remain,
and crush the rest out on your thigh.

NDABA SIBANDA

Sibanda is the author of *Notes, Themes, Things And Other Things, The Gushungo Way, Sleeping Rivers, Love O'clock, The Dead Must Be Sobbing, Football of Fools, Cutting-edge Cache, Of the Saliva and the Tongue, When Inspiration Sings In Silence, The Way Forward, Sometimes Seasons Come With Unseasonal Harvests, As If They Minded:The Loudness Of Whispers, This Cannot Be Happening :Speaking Truth To Power, The Dangers Of Child Marriages:Billions Of Dollars Lost In Earnings And Human Capital, The Ndaba Jamela and Collections and Poetry Pharmacy.* Sibanda's work has received Pushcart Prize and Best of the Net nominations. Some of his work has been translated into Serbian.

Website: https://ndabasibanda.wordpress.com
Facebook: https://www.facebook.com/ndabajs1
Twitter: @loveoclockn

12 DAYS

On the twelfth day of Christmas
my happy honey sent me twelve heavy honeycombs
      with eleven live busy bees buzzing around
      hungrily l ploughed my mouth into them
and WOW! ten sharp stings were drilled into me in return
at nine o`clock l was whizzed to a funny family doctor
      who robotically administered eight jumping jabs
      on me without as much as a wink for his antics
l actually saw seven stars of dizziness with my naked eyes … and
slept
for six silent hours like a dull dumped puppy pumpkin
      upon waking up the love of my life was there
      softly smooching me five times per minute non-
      stop!
telling me four fake ways of dreaming sweet dreams
three ways of avoiding snoring silly like a noisy tractor!
      and two wayward ways of making us
      one happy couple on a Christmas Day

A WHITTENBERG

A Whittenberg is a Philadelphia native who has a global perspective. If she wasn't an author she'd be a private detective or a jazz singer. She loves reading about history and true crime. Her other novels include *Sweet Thang, Hollywood and Maine, Life is Fine, Tutored,* and *The Sane Asylum.*

HELD

I am held

        Not by a mother's tender embrace
        I am captive in a ship slicing through the ocean

I am held

        Not by a lover's passion but bound,
        Manacled by people with strange language, hair,

and skin
I am held

        Not transfixed my mind races,
        Searching to escape this spell.

I am held
Not for a crime
But by decree.
I am held

        Not to be released at ransom's payment,
        But to be contained by another owner, then

another.
I am held at fifteen years old, and I will be held

For life.

PASSING AS A MULATTO

Four sisters where playing, laughing
The lightest one bragged,
'If we were back in the day,
I would be house,'
Then pointed, 'and you
Would be house,'
Then pointed again. 'But yall two
Would be field.'

> The girl judged like an overseer
> She felt she could since
> She was practically
> A white person,
> Except for the fact
> She had two black parents

(Not all black is black
Not all black comes from cotton,
The ghetto, primitive jungles.)

> She spent in that winter,
> Passing as a mulatto,
> Showing her near white hands,
> Keeping her nappy hair
Under a scarf.

MIRIAM SAGAN

Miriam Sagan is the author of over thirty books of poetry, fiction, and memoir. Her most recent include *Bluebeard's Castle* (Red Mountain, 2019) and *A Hundred Cups of Coffee* (Tres Chicas, 2019). She is a two-time winner of the New Mexico/Arizona Book Awards as well as a recipient of the City of Santa Fe Mayor's Award for Excellence in the Arts and a New Mexico Literary Arts Gratitude Award. She founded and directed the creative writing program at Santa Fe Community College until her retirement. Her poetry was set to music for the Santa Fe Women's Chorus, incised on stoneware for a haiku pathway, and projected as video inside an abandoned grain silo in rural Itoshima.

Her blog is Miriam's Well: http://miriamswell.wordpress.com

UNSEASONABLE

snow in early autumn
in these mountains
when only a few leaves have turned

you leave a used
face mask
and a paper bag
of tomatoes
behind

how long we've lived
together, you and I
how easy — how difficult
to part

in this
unseasonable weather

JUDE BRIGLEY

Jude Brigley is Welsh. She has been a teacher, an editor and a performance poet. She is now writing more for the page. She has been published in various magazines, including *Ariel Chart*, *Otherwise Engaged*, and *Blue ink*, as well as having a chapbook, called *Labours*.

THYRATIA BATIS

The moth flew in my window
mistaking my blue wall for sky.

Its pattern gleamed gold
in bars of evening sunlight,

reminding me of a silk blouse:
pink flowers on black silk

you could have worn.
And for a stilled moment,

before the window breeze
tempted a graceful escape

 to Llynfi woods, I thought
of you and how this was

the most apposite shape
for you to transubstantiate.

KEEPER

In her last days, I would lift my mother's head in my hands,
placing her cranium on the pillow, as painstakingly
as a priest or a sculptor, feeling her bones
rest in the feathers, like a small boulder,
as my hands slipped away, and her with no voice
to acknowledge my awkward progress .

I was the child who tripped over chalk lines,
dropped my coins in the grating, slopped
my tea cup on the Sunday-best cloth.

As the nurse stooped to bandage her legs,
raw and crusted as a war hero's,
my mother's eyes observed without reproach,
as I let the bowl's soapy water lap
to the floor, staining the carpet.

EACH OF THEM COULD BE US

The campaigning abortionist students warn their peers
of abortion victim photos ahead.

With 1960s naivete, I expect a picture of a dead blonde
in a sleazy back-street, or a red-haired woman on social,
desperate as her children are bundled
into the back of a case-worker's car.

Or perhaps, a stark picture of a bruised older woman
 raped on her way home, her assailant never identified,
or a young Catholic girl afraid to tell her mother
 of the 'shame' and her boyfriend
bound for the Americas or the mistress
 whose lover will never leave his wife
whatever the 'slip-up.'

It could be the young girl whose father
or uncle liked her that way and she can
never tell a family that loves those me,
and perhaps always knew but look away.

 Or the broken-hearted woman who hears
from those in white coats that her child
if born will never be normal and she knows
that back home she will be the one to blame.

And all of them confused, suffering,
marked by the moment
when legs open and life is never simple.

But no, these are not the pictures I see.
And as a woman, I need no warning
of blood or cords or unfinished labour,

But wonder where are the protests for the born?
For the children torn by war, wracked by starvation,
dying without medicine or those just down
the road in a leaking house,
gorging on junk food or shivering in fears?

And I think Dante should have a special circle
of hell for the self-righteous and how quick
we are to forget about first stones and judging.

COMPLEXITY

The front room was my grandmother's forte,
kept only for a grand occasion or visitor.
Her prizes - the china cabinet and upright piano,
unplayed since my mother was a girl.

Until my father found the record player
in the attic and the sarcophagus silence
was broken by Sinatra and Astaire.
And we were gifted the legacy to listen

to the wind-up music while the family watched
 television in the cramped middle room,
the sound deafening for my grandad's miner's ear,
while the parlour vibrated with syncopation.

So we sung along, dancing wildly to Winifred Atwell,
pretending to be prairie winds or rain pattering.
until Bing exhorted heaven for the fall of snow
And grabbing the winter globe we shook the flakes

passing the world between us but missing a beat
it slipped shattering ice on the tiled grate.
Frozen for a moment, we listened to see
who would come hammering while the 78

stopped its flourish and revolved on the deck.
        A handkerchief held the water and snow.
        No half-step or damper stopped our momentum.
We shoved the pieces under the abandoned piano,

safe in the knowledge no adult hand
could squeeze there. Each time we left,
we slipped a piece in a pocket, dispensing
the evidence, aware of the piano's quiet disapproval.

Later, sensing the pianissimo of complicity,
      we slipped notes and objects in its fallboard,
safe in the feeling that amongst its sharps and flats
our masterworks would not be played.

ZUBAIR JAVAID

REMINDING THE GOD

There it came- a ray of light saying bye to the ever burning sun and pushing throw the air, fleeting in glee curious of entering and lightening the valley of Kashmir. Travelling the infinity, it witnesses the scene of valley surrounded by the mountains, surface strewn with the glistening snow and few people roaming in Pherans.

Its eyes glued on a village_naked walnut trees wearing the gown of snow, The birds sorting pieces of wood in littered bullet shells on the desolate roads and busy weaving their nests, a murder of crows searching for their summer-stored walnuts in debris of houses.

The ray - confused of finding any standing house. Murmuring to itself "Maybe the chilly gust of 'Chilly kalan' are blurring my vision".

Shivering and roaming in cold, it finally sees a standing shed roofed with rusty tin and sieve like wall with holes on almost its every brick, maybe because of bullets, "Who knows" whispering to itself, the tired ray wafts in air towards it and enters the house through one of these holes. Sitting on the rusty nail holding calender, the ray of light notices the Inside of room_ Calm and quite, a woman leans by the wall, her head resting on her own shoulder like Chinar leaf on its own branch. Tear droplets hanging on the corners of her eyes reluctant of blinking. Holding "kangri" under her "Pheran" and photo of her Disappeared son clenched in her hands.

Sudden blast sound outside shakes the house except the woman in there, and the ray falls off the nail with a jerk and dips directly into her right eye and slips into the hanging tear droplet. The ray gets caught and lost in that universe of a tear droplet, hopes burried into its land, the surface strewn with ashy dreams, the desperate clouds showering memories of her son, the air-raucous with the slogans, wails and sounds of bullets and bombs. All this universe existing in just one tear droplet of that mother, who lost her son- the hope and happiness of her life. The universe and Its environment ripped apart the patience and body of ray. The ray struggling to come out of this unknown strange universe, yet the gravity of hopelessness pulls it back to the land of ashy memories.

The God perhaps sees the flickering ray, its innocence getting tormented. So the woman blinks and the universe of tear droplet rolls down in air, splashes to the surface throwing the half alive ray out of it. The ray realising the tragedy and pain of this paradise collects its breathe and strength and jumps with all the life left and strikes a glass surface reflecting it back to the air, before leaving it stops for a time being and glances back at the haunted valley_ where ghosts move with guns in streets, its deceptive view_ its air spreading rumours of peace and snow seeping into and escaping this dreadful place through the core of earth.

Its body torn, its light flickering, it return back to its origin, ignoring the sun for a cause, it wafts with sheer pace through the layers and layers and layers of vastness, traveling no way yet a way in itself, it passes through the planets, the stars, the galaxies ripping apart the shield of darkness, passing through the tough space of nothingness and travels for years carrying the pleas of that woman, the pain of her perhaps-killed son to God.

Travelling the infinity for ages it reaches some divine place. In it the arrays and arrays of rays- some full lit and some half, all crowded and crying the same pleas in same tone. Joining them, the never ending mob of rays cry out the ignored pleas, the ignored prayers of a helpless valley.

 The storm of rays, lightening the whole cosmos, all demanding the justice for valley and yelling in synchronized voice the slogans. The word "Azaadi" echoing everywhere in all galaxies, the stars, the moons, the planets and in the ear of that mother. The sound of fainting echoes blended with the sudden knocking sound at the door woke her up.

The sound as if knocking her heart not the door, its beats going high. She struggles to stand and approaches and open the door wide open. Her son with torcher marks on all his face, his clothes ripped apart like his childhood stood there in front of her.

Her mother sighing in shock, this long awaited knock, the sound of her triumphant. Touching her blood torn beautiful son, she hugs him , the tears dripped down her cheeks and hitted the ground, hundred of universes collapsing in seconds as she weeps. The rays in divinity scatter away their light and die in glee and the sound of pleas and slogans now faint, leaving the galaxies silent, dark and peaceful again.

ZAINAB WRITES FOR HER BELOVED POET:

O' people when i die, forget not, to write his poems on my shroud, when my cold body is being wrapped with it.

When my tomb is being taken out to graveyard through the bombarded lanes , Recite his poems until you put me into the lap of grave.

O' people write his poems on the epitaph of my grave,
when on it, your write my name,
forget not to write his pen name with it
And When you pray for me, read his poems, his words shall outdo the sound of bombs and bullets and bless my soul.

O' people when he dies, grab a fist of soil from his grave and scatter it on mine.
uproot some flowers from his grave and plant them on mine.
the perfume of flowers of our graves shall mix , live and saunter the haunted valley of kashmir together.

When his pen and paper finishes, tell him that i shall weep and bleed for years to fill his pen and after i die, tell him to dip a finger on the soil of my grave and write.

When thoughts of my death makes him upset, tell him that, i live in between the stanzas of his poems,
That when his pen and paper shall meet, we shall meet.

O' people when he hates his life after im gone, Tell him
My soul dances at the beats of his heart

that his breathe shall fly me higher and higher in the sky of his heart,
That i shall swim in his blood and in veins. That our memories shall live in his tears.

O' people tell him to visit the castle of my grave daily, and in curfew, when the barbed wires on roads and hopes stop him,
Tell him to write his words on chinar leaves, and the gusts of "chily kalan" shall guide them to my grave.

And when the ghosts with guns snatch his pen, tell him to whisper his words to the snowflakes and they, they shall seep directly into my grave, adsorb and embrace my shroud and his poems and love shall reach you.

O' the creator, when the ghosts with guns finish hanging and killing all the alive people of my land, and when they head towards our graveyards

Tell them to hang our Skeletons together. To crush our Skeletons together, So our dust roams together, the desolated valley of empty graves forever.

MAEVE M^CKENNA

Maeve McKenna lives in Sligo, Ireland. Her poetry has been placed in several international poetry competitions and published in *Mslexia, Bloody Amazing Anthology, Culture Matters Working Class prose Anthology; From The Plough To The Stars, The Cormorant, The Galway Review, Boyne Berries, MadSwirl, Sonder Magazine, Skylight47, Fly On The Wall* and widely online. She has work forthcoming in *Atrium, 100 Words Of Solitude* and *Black Bough*. Maeve is working towards her first collection of poetry.

BAT

Bat you are crying, furtive swoop,
a winged fox propelled by thin membrane;
your nocturnal jaunt kaleidoscopes of black spines

abandoned on a roof of skylines. The delicacy
of a butterfly's flight pirouettes
airborne towards the recoiled leaf of a rose bush,

tinctures of flamboyant disguise unsettle
like the rattle of deaths bedtime. All is frail
within us. Forms span and merge, dilute, a tempting

palette of dual deception that snares
like a vice, each elusive promise a cobweb
of finely spun voice. Drastic this silent hunger,

uproar inside chambers of grief
that summon each perilous journey of blood loss
inside the ravenous animal of night.

JB MULLIGAN

JBMulligan has published more than 1100 poems and stories in various magazines over the past 45 years, and has had two chapbooks: *The Stations of the Cross* and *THIS WAY TO THE EGRESS*, as well as 2 e-books: *The City of Now and Then*, and *A Book of Psalms* (a loose translation). He has appeared in more than a dozen anthologies.

PEOPLES IS A CURIOUS AMINAL

I

Voices, crying out in the tameness,
"Surely we were meant
for drudgery such as this."
But the spirit beats on the bars,
orders another drink, and laughs
loudly, a desperate trumpet
announcing the postponement of defeat.

II

The icon in the gilt-edged mirror,
with chips of yellow paint and wood
like petals of a lost parade around him,
smiles, beneficent and wise,
holding forth gems of opinion
like relics of a dream
that mattered, once.

III

Trading is brisk,
the profits small;
the marketplace is filled
with hungry mouths
and dried-up teats.

IV

Utterances drift like smoke -

so I told him
but you said
craziest fucking thing I ever
people are strange
what can you say
and the wind of tomorrow
waits outside the door
like a stranger's dog.
Inside, the bones
wipe mouths, consider tips.
Silver flashes. Crumpled green.

V

The undertow of music
from the back of the bar -
"I could be happy
the rest of my life."

Dududuh dum dum -
fists on the bar,
the drums of imagination,
the disconnected tribe.

"I need another chance."
The hidden feet agree.

Quotes in section V from Neil Young, "Cinnamon Girl"

VEGETAL

i

The vegetal dangle of houseplants
from the living room ceiling:
medusan heads
as we turn to stone, slowly,
from seeing nothing
and the recognition.

The putative calm of a tank
of tropical fish. Bubbles
tumble endlessly up
from the filter. A flash of red -
the flame gourami, male,
roaming his sterile,
rectangular sea.

ii

Mike is dead - shot
a block from the bar he ran
two decades ago
for preppies learning to drink.
He bought us rounds,
extended credit

to kids he didn't know.
No suspects in the shooting.
He always smiled.
I leaned against the jukebox,

learning to watch
what people do for love.

iii

A pleco darts to the surface,
spits bubbles - flops to the bottom.
The air pump hums.
The rain outside is soft
scratching on glass.
He always smiled;

I wonder if he knew
his killer. The pleco suctions
algae from glass,
flaring the silk of his fins.
The houseplants extend
such verdant promises.

ICHABOD'S PRIZE

A toy in the mouth
of our youngest cat -
no, a living toy,
a mouse, in silhouette
its eye an eight ball
shiny in barroom light
waiting to be sunk.

My wife and son and I
chase Ichabod
off the fridge,
onto the counter,

I haven't seen
a mouse in a while.
The grey of its coat
is vivid in a way
I didn't recall.
A military grey.

Is this a new game?,
the cat wonders,
'cause if it is
it's stupid
this is A MOUSE!

At last we get them
split, and chase off
Ichabod
with a water gun.

It takes ten minutes
and a can of food
to calm him down.

The mouse we bring
outside. It isn't
calm. It runs.

You can't explain
knowing you'll die
to something that's alive
until the present stops
(which Ichabod did
four months later:
something preyed
on his red blood cells,
something he couldn't escape).

All you can do
is squirt it, feed it,
and finally get
your cup of coffee,
a couple of doughnuts,
and start the day again.

JOHN LAMBREMONT

John Lambremont, Sr. is a poet and writer from Baton Rouge, Louisiana, where he lives with his wife and their little dog. John holds a B.A. in Creative Writing and a J.D. from Louisiana State University. He is the former editor of *Big River Poetry Review*, and has been nominated for The Pushcart Prize. John's poems have been published internationally in many reviews and anthologies, including *Pacific Review*, *Flint Hills Review*, *The Minetta Review*, *Sugar House Review*, and *The Louisiana Review*. John's full-length poetry collections include *"Dispelling The Indigo Dream"* (Local Gems Poetry Press 2013), *"The Moment Of Capture"* (Lit Fest Press 2017), *"Old Blues, New Blues"* (Pski's Porch Publishing 2018), and *"The Book Of Acrostics"* (Truth Serum Press 2018). His chapbook is *"What It Means To Be A Man (And Other Poems Of Life And Death)"*, published in 2014 by Finishing Line Press. John enjoys music, playing his guitars, fishing, and old movies. He has battled pancreatic cancer since 2018.

A MAN AND HIS MUSE

A man studies poetry writing in college,
then leaves his poems behind
to pursue a graduate degree
in a more lucrative calling.

After a thirty-year hiatus,
he returns to writing creatively,
as he has some things to say
before he passes his time.

He thus turns to nature,
experiences, relationships, art, music,
literature, science, myth and legend,
history, popular culture, and religion.

Sometimes he finds inspiration,
and writes poems.
Other times, he doesn't.

THE BACKWARD ATTACKER

an acrostic

Each branch he sits on is usually sheared off,
Diversity his curse, not a blessing,
Will attack larger crows, hawks, and owls,
Aggressive in his aerial pursuit of flies,
Razor-sharp tail feathers split in two,
Deeply cut those who disturb his nest.

Scythe twins protrude from his rear end,
Cane knives work best inverted,
Is able to advance in reverse,
Strange this kingbird compared to all others,
Scares off many potential mates,
Oscillating blades like a table fan,
Rotate in either direction,
Tyrannus forficatus at its most bizarre,
A unique member of a flock of thousands,
In flight trying not to clip a neighbor's wing,
Long way to Panama from Oklahoma.

LISHA RUAN

Lisha Ruan lives and writes in New York. Her hobbies include learning languages and reading philosophy. Her work has appeared in *The Bitter Oleander* and other journals.

Twitter: @lisha_ruan

RIVER

The cloves fall like lengths
onto a sea's spray

Bark like a nacreous apple
phases the dusks in the dew

A sunny star contends the stomachs
on a dancing red oath

The hurts go like grass musks
to the rose of a wine

FLOW

cold flow
almond as the apple
deals like hands

hurts fall like cloves
on a grave aftermark

EMPTY

empty as the salt
loves rust like lengths
before a frozen wine

on a weak joy
hands sign like diamonds

RACHEL DEVEREAUX

Rachel is a transformational nurse coach who helps busy people make life easier. With health, wellbeing and practical tips Rachel is able to help you life edit and feel good. Her books are helping parents with difficult conversations and life events. Contact Rachel via www.racheldevereux.com

THERE WAS A BABY

A poem for Rainbow children to learn about their siblings who died through miscarriage or stillbirth.

There was a baby in mummy's tummy
For some reason they didn't stay

There was a baby in mummy's tummy
I don't know why they went away

There was a baby in mummy's tummy
Born so quiet and still

There was a baby in mummy's tummy
A space in my heart for them to fill

There was a baby in mummy's tummy
I get sad to think they died

There was a baby in mummy's tummy
A lot of tears I have cried

There was a baby in mummy's tummy
Before you were alive

There was a baby in mummy's tummy
Unlike you they did not survive

There was a baby in mummy's tummy
A sibling of yours called…..

There was a baby in mummy's tummy
We can remember them today

There was a baby in mummy's tummy
A sibling you never knew

There was a baby in mummy's tummy
I know they'd have really loved you.

Previously published as a children's picture book by Inside Out Publishing (2019)

AYESHA ASIM

My name is Ayesha Asim. I am 13 years old. One of the things i love to do it poetry and digital art. They are my hobby as well as passion and thats it hope you will like my work.

FLYING

I was trying to fly higher
By the wings you gave me
But you cut them off
By saying that they weren't made for me
I started running and realised
Even if you run instead of flying
One day you will reach your destination
It's just running will take you more time than flying
But you will reach your destiny
Then it doesn't matter if you came by running or flying

TIFFANY LINDFIELD

Tiffany Lindfield is a social worker by day, trade, and heart working as an advocate for climate justice, gender equality, and animal welfare. By night, she is a prolific reader of anything decent, and a writer.

Website: https://www.tiffanylindfield.com
Facebook: https://www.facebook.com/authortiffanylindfield

THE WIND SINGS

Leaves rustle and branches wave.
The wind hasn't a tongue to
Roll Rrrrs.
Perrrrro/a is the same as puppy, and/or bitch.
Plastic rattles gripped in the hands of babies,
Screaming. Their teeth haven't broken the gums,
But their diaphragm expands,
Room needed for bellowing.

The wind sweeps, collecting molecules,
And trace elements.
To carry across many landscapes,
Over water making ripples.
The earliest hieroglyphics:
Squiggly, wiggly lines.
Wave is the same as something coming.
Squint to hear.

The wind lacks a pharynx, but it
Sings through the wind chime.
Silver tubing, bamboo shoots,
Clanking glass, and seashells.
Via the medium of trees, leaves,
Wispy strands of hair in an elephant's ear,
Crashing waves over the back of whales, the
Wind blows and blusters about.

MARTINA GALLEGOS

Martina was born and raised in Mexico and came to the United States at 14. She attended California State University, Northridge and became a bilingual elementary school teacher and taught for almost eighteen years. She suffered a work injury in 2012, followed by a near fatal hemorrhagic stroke. She got a Master's degree from Grand Canyon University and started publishing after surviving her stroke. Her works have appeared in the *Altadena Poetry Review: Anthology 2015*, *Spirit Fire Review*, *Silver Birch Press*, *Central Coast Poetry Shows*, *Poetry Superhighway*, *Poets Responding to SB1070*, *Hometown Pasadena*, and *Basta!*

Instagram: @Selbor2015
Website: www.martinagallegos.com
Facebok: https://www.facebook.com/martina.gallegos.188

DOUBLE-WHAMMY

He is one of the essentials, the fieldworker
who awakens before the mockingbird,
to harvest the food that feeds America.
He's the essential who puts his life on the line
so others can enjoy a healthy meal
with their families,
but he can't spend five minutes with his.
He's the essential worker with no benefits
to help his own family through COVID
or any other emergency.
He's the one others call illegal,
even though he'd much rather be called undocumented
because no human being is illegal.
He's the immigrant used as a scapegoat
for the ills of society
nobody takes responsibility for.
The pandemic is the great equalizer
that is now reaching America's fieldworkers
who are not supposed to get sick.
Now it's the time for the patriots
to run to the fields and rescue
the food that feeds America.
Somehow, though, patriots lose their way
to the fields but never their hatred
for the true heroes who feed them.

A NATION ON EDGE

Three days after Election Day,
Liar-in-Chief is spewing more lies than ever
and is creating more hate and division than ever.
He gave a speech that fell on deaf ears
because for once, some networks showed some decency
and spared the nation of malignant lies.
He was in the Briefing Room, claiming the usual: voting by mail
is a fraud;
the Democrats are stealing the election.
He claimed victory before votes were counted
then screamed, "Stop the votes!" "Stop counting!"
He's filing lawsuits left and right, but mostly Ultra-Right,
to stop vote counting and defraud the nation,
and he's riling up his blind base,
who are violence and blood thirsty
to feed the wishes of their cult leader.
Those guys, you know, the fine people Liar-in-Chief always
praises,
are blindly but willingly projecting the vile
wishes of their cultist leader who cares not about the country,
but only about his narcissistic self
and doesn't care who he destroys.
The voting public is glued to their television
waiting anxiously for every blue sliver
knocking on democracy,
and it slowly begins to breathe again
despite a tsunami of hateful vitriol.
The waves of democracy, although small,
shall come out victorious.

A NATION SIGHS A SIGH OF RELIEF

The slivers of red turned into democratic blues
and gave democracy its life back once more,
and the nation and the world sigh a collective
and well-deserved sigh of relief.
The masses once more hit the streets nationwide,
but this time to celebrate and praise to the heavens
that decency and dignity reign with democracy.
There's hopeful suspense for a peaceful transition
that the incumbent occupier refuses to guarantee
and straight out has said he won't concede
but instead promises to fight baseless battles
that will instead engrave a capital L on his forehead
and continue to be the laughing stock of the world.

BETTER LIFE MATTERS

Isn't life just grand?
Look around you: people are celebrating everywhere.
The pandemic is just icing on the cake;
people are dropping like flies, but don't worry,
it's almost nothing, and holding rallies is more important
than consoling those who lost loved ones.
Don't worry if you get COVID either;
you can go to the best hospital taxpayers can pay for
so you can hold big parties and brag about
your super strength and life-time immunity;
you know, the guy that begs women to "please like me."
Your supporters swallow your every fake word,
and you tell them not to be intimidated
by the China Virus,
but the world now knows it by Trump's Virus,
the deadliest of all viruses.
But now that you were allegedly struck by COVID,
you're the top expert all must listen to.
Better life matters to people with a conscience,
but it doesn't matter to the biggest cheater in the universe
who is the puppet to another crook meddling
in the elections to re-elect the fool once more.
IQ45 is going out on a limb to make sure
he steals the elections like he did before,
and he's inciting violence against
people who differ from his political opinions,
and it's ok for "oh, those guys" to attempt against
the life of the opposite party.
Bet you he wouldn't feel the same way it it were
the other way around.

Bet you the other side wouldn't even be allowed peaceful
assemblies.
They'd all be stashed away in for-profit prisons owned
and run by his own cronies.
He expects to claim victory on election day
because he doesn't care for the will of the people
and has neither loyalty nor respect for country or Constitution.
May history remember him for the poisonous excrement
that the world knows him to be,
and may the country soon heal from his treasonous acts.
May democracy be victorious
for a better life for the nation.

CAN YOU HEAR ME?

Hey, God, can you hear me?
How silly of me, but of course you can.
Tell me, what's your plan for me?
Why do you still have me here?
Maybe I'm not supposed to ask questions,
but if I don't ask, I will not know.
My mind is puzzled beyond words;
I know I doubt you,
but it's because of the contradictions I see.
Maybe I should say I question you;
I want to know if I understand
how your mind really works.
What kind of mind does a god have?
Is that even a question to ask?
I don't think I've asked for much;
I only want to understand
what's happening to our world.
This seems to be a theme in my life:
If you make all things happen,
why let children be witnesses to war?
And why allow wars to happen in the first place?
Mother Nature is crying tears of pain;
she's losing her children to neglect,
and mankind simply sits by and stares.
Hey, God, you've watched my every sleepless night;
you've heard my pleas for peace for Planet Earth.
Why is money more important than human dignity?
It wouldn't be too much bother,
if you'd just grant a wish or two
and put this doubter's heart at ease.

DOUGLAS K CURRIER

Douglas K Currier has published work in many magazines both in the United States and in South America. He lives with his wife in Carlisle, Pennsylvania.

REST,

as in day of,
the pause that
finishes the week.
I have not been to church
in a month of.
I do not congregate. I believe
in residual grace and
extenuating circumstances.

We enter foreign churches
out of nostalgia,
for the museums
they are – envy and pity
the small ladies in black
that worship there,
all the theres we've been.

Reliquia, marble and bone,
hand-hewn timbers, holy
water, candles, the grave
graves of saints, donation
boxes – always a bird or two
trapped by the high, skyward
ceilings and the silent chill.

A WAY THAT COUNTS

Let me tell you that I am old,
old in a way that counts – not
just years, but old in people,
places, lost things, empty things,
the dead, regret. I am the portrait
behind the bathroom mirror
and no diminishment of light,
no window or shaded lamp,
changes that. I am older
than character, the receding
residue of youth rinsed from sink.
I am the "nothing much to lose."
I am the thin white legs that rock
themselves out of the bed.

Years are nothing but make-believe.
I am "once upon a time" old.
I am the thoughtless, measureless
old of dust. I am my next slight illness,
my last pair of clean socks.

GEORGE HIGHAM

George Higham started writing poetry at 59, in the Summer of 2020. He is from North Wales and currently lives South East England.

Instagram: @ageing_dreamer

WANDERING FREE

Little by little life passes by
Just wandering around below the sky
A spot of rain splashes there
I wonder around without a care

Strolling along just with myself
With my book I took from my bookshelf
Sitting down under a tree
Just enough sun so I can see

Reading the story in my book
I just happened to look up
I saw a stranger pass me by
Out of the corner of my eye

The stranger passed and threw me a smile
I wondered afterwards for a while
That was a lovely thing to do
When a stranger can just smile at you

My book I picked I'd already read
The cover had a title in red
I stood from where I sat under the tree
Away in the distance I could see

More people wandering without a care
There wasn't many people there
The sun was setting behind the trees
The evening was chilly with a slight breeze

I decided it was time to go
So off I wandered nice and slow
Another end to another day
It was lovely wandering around today.

JOHN CARTER

John Carter attended Old Dominion University, where he earned degrees in a number of esoteric subjects. He works when he must and lives where he can. He is currently at work on his first collection of poems, entitled *Earth Is Not The Best Planet*.

TURTLES

All the way down
is
probably best
even given the lack of privacy
an infinity of turtles
would involve

one above
one below
always and forever.

But
think of the alternative

one turtle
its shell straining under the
slow turtle despair
of
who knows how many
turtles
stacked above

and nothing but abyss below.

No one could blame that
final
turtle
for staring straight down and

moaning
enough enough already.

ANOTHER STAGE OF GRIEF

Already
no one can agree.
I say her skin was white
as startled doves
but
the others shake their heads.

No
porcelain definitely porcelain
they argue.

And yesterday
we were sure
her lipstick was pomegranate
but now
grave doubt exists.

And even her garden.
I claim
(tongue-in-cheek to be honest)
that she grew gigantic
ten foot
venus fly traps
penitent for
their nerveless crimes.

Imagine her after a full week
dead.
My good god.

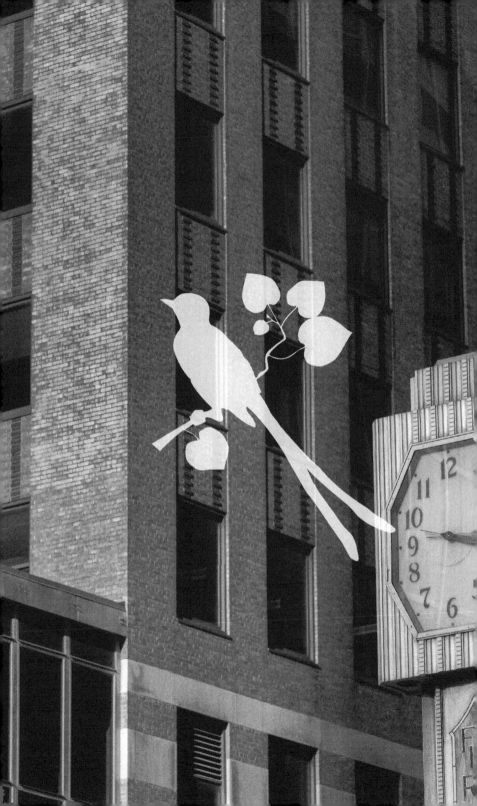

Printed in Poland
by Amazon Fulfillment
Poland Sp. z o.o., Wrocław

65758362R00078